To C

Little memo
for you

Also many many
thanks for pushing
travel my way.

Love
Roy

# THERE AND BACK AGAIN

Roy Norcliffe

Roy Norcliffe, 5 Austhorpe Gardens,
Leeds, LS15 8TF, West Yorkshire, UK

# THERE AND BACK AGAIN

## All Rights Reserved

ISBN Number 0-9537612-0-7

First Published  2000
'Journey'
5 Austhorpe Gardens
Leeds
LS15 8TF
West Yorkshire, UK

Printed in Great Britain by Unity Print Ltd

# THERE AND BACK AGAIN

# FOREWORD

Travel is both wondrous and fun.  Being able to reflect
with humour these trag-comic events keeps their
memories consistently vivid.
This book is for those of you who, like me, can laugh
uproariously at themselves.

*Dedicated*

To all the friends I've made, and to all those who've shared the fun.....

To my wife June for keeping much of this in perspective!

# ACKNOWLEDGEMENTS

I wish to thank the Administrative colleagues – my special friends Nina, Debbani, Cathy and Lynn – at the College for their painstaking preparation of the manuscript and the numerous people who encouraged me to put 'good stories' into print.

# THERE AND BACK AGAIN

**Contents**

# Chapter 1

# INTRODUCTION

## *BLACKPOOL*

I suppose it all began for me as a babe in arms, the war years, variety shows, sand and ice-cream – often at the same time - Blackpool Tower and the Pleasure Beach.

Dad was a miner which meant one holiday week per year, in August, and another week when we had all gone back to school in September, usually Doncaster St. Leger Race Week. Mum was a chronic diabetic - a serious illness in the 1940's, but Blackpool air, flat terrain and bustle appeared to make her thrive.

I clearly remember the routine - breakfast, beach, Pablo's for an ice-cream, beach, a ride on Fairyland with three pence obtained from deckchair deposits, lunch, beach, Fairyland, tea, a magnetic show somewhere, then supper and bed - 6 consecutive days of exactly the same routine. But how we loved it! Joseph Locke, Jewel and Warriss, George Formby, Elsie and Doris Waters, Frank Randall. Mesmeric, glittering, merely voices from the radio, but brought to unbelievable real life for a few fleeting minutes.

Booking these shows was also routine. A full Sunday morning spent in huge queues, but three hours later or so, back would come Dad - usually with seven shows booked, and this for his family of four. The cost - I haven't a clue!

4

Usually talk in the Pataline Road boarding house would feature this show or that, this act or that – the shocking Frank Randall who used the word "bloody" in his act, the statuesque topless beauties who graced Joseph Locke's show – it was beginning to happen even then. But first night was inevitably the Circus.

The weather - invariably superb.  Swimming midst the condoms and sanitary towels, emboldened by a brisk donkey ride and Punch and Judy repartee, we could take on the world, and often had to, simply to secure three square yards of beach by the Central Pier. Where <u>did</u> we all come from?  Mostly by train I would suspect.

Leave Sheffield; change at Barnsley - why Barnsley God only knows - change again at Manchester, eventually sixpence from Dad for the first one to see the Tower some 4/5 hours later. (However even this did not compare to 1948 - 8 hours from Sheffield to Scarborough).

The pushing and shoving, snarls and grunts from Dad, more profound and obvious insults and pointers from Mum we had a whale of a time, rushing on and off these trains. Arriving one year (1942) we found that our boarding house had been commissioned by the RAF, so night one was spent under the North Pier; but Mum and Aunty soon rectified this - Captain or no, he had to go, as did others, to make way for the Norcliffes.

Did these superlative holidays embracing our whole saved up Winter's sweet ration, giddy Pleasure Beach rides, long promenade walks, beautiful boarding house waitresses ( or so they seemed to a 9 year old) pave the way for the sophistication and extraordinary events of years to come?

The memories remain evocative, the sense of smell and sound, particularly those unique tram noises still the same today as then. Returning now only occasionally with Grand-children or to Crown Green Bowl, visions of those marvellous days return to haunt.

Was it Blackpool which first evoked in me the love of the Theatre and the ability to act, direct, teach and ultimately lecture in the Performing Arts? Remembering those long gone Music Hall stars, seeing Wilfred Pickles as Willie Mossop in 'Hobsons Choice' at the Opera House were pure unadulterated hours of joy. Bits and bobs of memories come floating back - forgive the indulgence, let's move on to more modern times and some 'there and back agains' in foreign climes.

# Chapter 2

# £35.00 ! ! ! ?

It was a dark gloomy February day in 1989 when the decision was made to 'try' the Orient Express and furthermore to go the whole distance to Venice. Nothing controversial about this, expensive, ultimately found to be overrated, as it was. Nevertheless a unique experience of which I intend to espouse very little. No, it was the peripheries which were so astonishing in their outcomes; and as we duly confirmed our London to Venice booking on the O.E. so our minds began to examine more pretentious and ambitious targets. After all we had two full weeks at our disposal so why not go on to Istanbul, taking local trains and then flying back home? Nothing could be simpler, and so as we booked the Orient Express, dutiful wife went to the Leeds station continental booking office to comply with the recently taken decisions.

"Not taking bookings yet" said the brusque elegantly attired male representative behind the counter.

"Come back in another month" he disarmingly told her.

Well, yours truly went back about 14 days later, and without ado was booked onto the Venice-Belgrade evening train and from there another overnight train to Istanbul passing through Yugoslavia, Bulgaria and so into Turkey. The overnight journey offering routine sleepers.

"I'll pay by Visa Card" - I instructed the Leeds British Rail know it all.

"Right - £35.00" came the response.

"£35.00 - that's cheap - all the way for 35.00, are you sure?" A look of pain crossed the man's features.

"Sir - Continental travel is exceptionally cheap, you must realise that"!

"Well er--er-- yes I suppose so but check again will you 'cos I can't believe my luck?"

£35.00 was duly confirmed and tickets eventually issued. Well this certainly compensated for the heavy cost of the O.E., and later during Easter 1989, we eventually arrived in Venice after an interesting if somewhat routine start to the holiday.

On each of our 3 evenings in Venice we checked platform numbers and times, and their consistency was encouraging except of course when it became our turn on the 4th evening; with no signs of the Belgrade train some 40 mins before departure time.

"No problem" explained a more than helpful station officer.

"You take the Trieste train, change there and into Belgrade in good time" - we anticipated some 6 hours or so here to explore the City next day.

Settled comfortably into our seats accompanied by 3 Swiss nuns, 3 Italians and goodness knows what other totally non-speaking English companions, all seemed reasonably well set - Not so!!!!

The ticket collector took one look at my tickets and began to mutter - obviously in Italian - his mutterings rising to crescendo, then to near apoplexy as no-one -, but no-one - in that compartment could explain to us the problems we were so innocently causing. With a final headshake, more verbals and histrionics we caught the word "Trieste" and sincerely hoped all would indeed be explained on the next train. Smiling stupidly, nodding and winking to our now most alert companions we kept separate counsel until Trieste. But from the back of my mind the words "only £35.00" would insist on forcing themselves to the fore!

Trieste. A smiling good natured conductor; great he could speak English - and the explanation was unbelievably and blindingly obvious.

"Oh sir. They have sold you *sleeping* accommodation for the trains but not *tickets* for the train, you shouldn't really be aboard! But no problem, pay now and then buy tickets in Belgrade for the next leg".

Right! Out came the necessary English sterling and everyone now satisfied, we awoke in Belgrade at about 8am the following morning just prior to our arrival. But we still needed to purchase tickets to complement our sleeper bookings. This proved a tediously long term process at the enquiry desk, and at the Belgrade bank because Yugoslavian currency was imperative for the fare. Ever tried handling about £45.00 in Yugoslavian currency? Well a paper-boys' bag would be the best receptacle for such a 'wodge' of money, even if it was only carried from the bank to the station. But it was duly managed and most of it deposited over the counter. By this time a general walk in the city, a MacDonald's and a toilet stop where even more virtually useless currency, approximately 3/4" thick was added to the wallet. (This as change for a note worth about 10p, took us to departure time).

It surely must be all straightforward from now on in? But no, the worst was yet to come. Nightfall, a stop at the Bulgarian border, and the dreaded words from our new German travelling companion - a youngster of about 20 yrs.

"Oh this is where they will want to see your passports and *Visa*?"

"Visa! what Visa?"

"The Visa you need to enter Bulgaria".

"But I'm not entering Bulgaria, I'm passing through it, who wants to jump train in Bulgaria?"

"You'll still need a visa or hard currency, Deutchsmarks, Dollars, Francs, Sterling"

"But I've only Turkish money now" Panic, panic, panic.

By this time along came a Mr Peter Sellers look alike. Black hat, black gloves, black great-coat - thrown over one shoulder - black leggings, black boots, black everything it seemed to us - the Devil Incarnate. Just try explaining to a character like this and his two similarly unsmiling sidekicks that you've no visa and no currency - Furthermore he is not remotely interested in the prat at British Rail Leeds who put you in this mess.

"You British" he stormed "always out to cause trouble" ----- - the rest I lost in another storm of abuse.

"What happens now?! I asked my wide-eyed German friend,

"Well you <u>could</u> be put off at the border - luggage and all" came his reassuring answer. Just the positive response I needed.

Brainwave - after all we were holding up a huge train .

"Can you lend us any marks to pay for two visas?"

However, before he could respond, our passports were taken away by Bulgarian Bill Mutt and Geoff and all these disappeared off the train, leaving us with that most distinctive of sinking feelings. There was not a lot worse then, of being passportless in an Eastern bloc country.

"Don't worry, yes, pay me back in Turkish money when we arrive in Istanbul".

Whereupon he gave me sufficient to meet the demands of Bulgarian Bill upon his return some 40 mins later. Were we popular? I've never had so many people waiting upon my every move.

That was really about the end of it; another passport check at the Turkish border, and having to offload the train. A further full inspection, for "cultural reasons", aboard the train, then final arrival in Istanbul and repayment of our debts to our priceless wonderful saviour.

The return journey was by far the less traumatic but still not devoid of incident. This journey, as already touched upon was by air and via an Eastern European Company which not only landed in Rumania (Bucharest) but in Vienna too on its way to Heathrow. Istanbul security at that time was brusquely efficient, our taxi driver and luggage not even negotiating first base - the airport doors - before being excluded from any further part in the proceedings. After some delay we then, for the first time in our extensive travel repertoire, had to identify our luggage dumped on the runway, before rejoining the considerable queue for boarding. A garrulous but splendid Rumanian engaged in earnest but interesting conversation with us actually forgot to identify his luggage and that caused additional confusion and fuss.

Once at the doors of the aircraft a further body search ensued, but for us Brits a wave of the old black passport was sufficient to eliminate this indignity. Changing over tickets in Budapest resembled a mad scramble for cup final tickets as it was patently obvious that availability did not match claimants. Therefore with great relief we were more than delighted when our names were called and we were able to reboard; this time to Vienna and then to home.

Remember how the Pope kisses the tarmac upon landing? We couldn't help empathising with how he feels when finally Heathrows' tarmac was below our feet.

## Chapter 3

# ROCKHAMPTON JAIL FOR YOU!

August 1988 first time in the Antipodes and destination Queensland, staying with friends at Sunnybank in the outlying modern red-brick district of Brisbane. Nothing unusual transpired at the outset and up to the midway point of the holiday where everything was exciting and tremendously invigorating. The newness of the experience meant long days, and even longer though darker nights, to savour it all, including very interesting visits to Expo.

It was decided to attempt our own mini-tour by driving North up Bruce Highway, the only arterial road directly linking the South East of Australia to the towns of the Greater Barrier Reef namely Bundaburg, Rockhampton, Mackay, Bowen, Townsville, Cairns and finally Cooktown.

Our vehicle was a hired new Toyota Camry, a superb, swish automatic vehicle with about 400 miles on the clock, sheer luxury for a man who'd just graduated from a 1977 Ford Escort.

Bundaburg, the heart of the sugar/rum making industry was the first port of call and nothing much to report here except perhaps the embarrassment of dialect misunderstanding, one of which evoked laughter the other which developed a long term friendship. Placing the school's video camera into the Camry boot in the Bundaberg hotel car park, a genial Aussie asked me how I 'Liked the Camry'.

'Not good' I responded 'it's getting old and my staff didn't treat it properly, always taking bits off to supplement another'. A blank look from the enquirer and a cocked eyebrow of puzzlement made me realise he was talking about the car and not the video recorder!

'Oh, sorry great, great car, smooth, comfortable, roomy, quick.'

How the word 'quick' was to haunt me within the next few days, on the return journey, but before then our destination was completed at Shute Harbour, where a Barrier Reef visit by air, including walking, snorkelling on the reef and a cruise around the Whitsunday Islands and sightseeing made the days enormously memorable.

Whilst on the Catamaran cruising round the islands, the painted letters 'DEIGHTON' on the video case which were somewhat faded I must confess, were interpreted by a lady on board as 'BRIGHTON'. A genuine case of confusion, but one which happily led to an animated conversation.

"Most people in Huddersfield don't know where Deighton is", I explained in answer to her question 'never mind me having to explain it to Australians'. Thus began a long term relationship to be resumed in the flesh this summer on the Sunshine Coast.

However, all this was well behind us of course as we motored South back down Bruce highway. Virtually empty roads, tiny villages, dead Kangaroos and miles and miles and miles of forests on either side. Try it, you will know what I mean.

With service stations literally hundreds of miles apart, it was almost compulsory to stop to fill up, feed up and put your feet up and this particular stop was some miles short of Rockhampton Town, being no more and no less like all the other stopovers. Of course these stations sell everything, but everything, and it was only with semi-interest that I watched a huge Stetson hatted 'cop' and his skinny side-kick wearing very dark sunglasses, mooch aimlessly about the place, both inside and outside checking on the cars, before driving off in their unmarked motor vehicle. (Dark glasses coming into my life again, I should have heeded the warning).

Duly replenished we'd travelled another couple of miles or so when, after rounding a steep bend we were 'shot' by a speed gun aimed by the previously discovered policemen.

Dark glasses leaned laconically in my open window. 'Know what speed you hit that bend at mister?'

No, I'd no idea, comfortably, smoothly easily I thought but visibly shaken I confessed to not knowing.

'Seventy four miles per hours mate' he replied, 'for that offence you could be taken and locked up in Rockhampton Jail – did you know that?'

Bit drastic I thought, but speechless with terror – the first time I'd been 'done' in 33 years of driving all over the world. I burbled something like. ' Superb car........didn't seem to be going fast......enjoying the scenery'..........actually that latter statement was a load of tripe, inspiring scenery it wasn't.

It transpired that the limit is a conservative 50 mph and the incongruity of it all were the miles of empty road, no people, vehicles, animals - apart from dead Kangaroos. I began to feel insulted.

'Anyway you're booked and you'd better pay up before you leave Australia or you won't be allowed back in again'. With that he rudely stuffed the ticket into my hand. Bit drastic all this seemed to me here out in the sticks and two country bumpkins, throwing their nasty weight about. Again over his shoulder 'Rockhampton Jail' was muttered.

At maximum, lawful, speed we resumed our journey, perhaps now better described via reading the following letters I later wrote to the Police which really says it all.

Multiplicity of conflicting advice when we arrived back in Brisbane, 'Forget it', 'pay it', 'rotten bastards', 'only doing a job', it was all there somewhere. However the letter, something of a cathartic process for me, was written, setting up a chain of processes while I was safely back ensconced in Leeds:

"25 August 1988

The Commissioner
Department of Transport
Transport House, Valley Plaza
230 Brunswick Street
FORTITUDE VALLEY. PO BOX 525
QLD 4006.  AUSTRALIA

Dear Sir

TRAFFIC OFFENCE NOTICE NO.4057046(4)

On the 9 August 1988 the above ticket was given to me.
Please find enclosed the sum of £36.00 calculated against
the current Australian Dollar exchange rate.  Please note
that I will require a receipt of this back in the UK.

Whilst I have no alternative but to accept the reading given
to me by your officer, I still have considerable doubts that
the speed shown was in fact accurate.  Looking back at the
bend behind which your officers were both 'hiding' I still
feel that to have negotiated that bend at the said speed of
124 kmh, qualifies me more as a Rally Drive than as a Head
Teacher.

It is ironic that this is my first motoring  offence in 33 years
of driving, many miles of which have been done throughout
the world.  On the Bruce highway, where there is mile after
mile of empty and safe road, free of pedestrians, traffic,
buildings, I consider the speed I was doing to be totally
sensible, safe and of no danger to fellow human beings.

Even more importantly, I would certainly consider my own driving to be infinitely better than the majority of road users in that part of the world, whose standards of overtaking particularly were very poor.

I also wonder, at a time when your Queensland Police Force is obviously very much in the public eye and claiming a great deal of media attention that you can afford to have, presumably, trained professionals with nothing better to do than catch unsuspecting motorists both in their unmarked car and in their places of 'hiding'. I have to say I found this an act of total cowardice. I also found it amazing that once stopped these two highly trained officers then found it necessary to follow me for a further 9 km at exactly100km speed, presumably in the forlorn hope of prosecuting me again. They may be good enough to await around a corner, they certainly were not good enough to remain unspotted travelling some 200 yds or so behind me, even in their unmarked car. It was also interesting that when they finally overtook me they had allowed a white van with local plates to then overtake them at speeds well in excess of 110 kms and do nothing about it, except to make a dangerous complete turn-about in the main road and head off back where they came from. I respectfully suggest that these two officers need something better to do with their time.

Again, your officers' attitude left much to be desired in terms of visitors, who enjoyed a superb four weeks stay in Queensland and who make no excuses for doing the wrong thing in terms of speed limit. You will also realise that as I am now safely back in the UK it would be very easy to throw your notice in the bin without your being able to do much about it. However I do not believe that this is the right thing to do and that I do owe a debt. I also understand that the financial situation in your state is not good. If I can be of any assistance then every little helps!

I conclude by repeating that a friendly word of warning, a more sensitive attitude and a greater trust from your officers would certainly have deterred me and that I would have been far more careful with my speed, despite during our 3,000 + km trip spending most of this driving in splendid isolation.

Yours faithfully,

Roy Norcliffe – Headteacher BEd (Hons. ADB(Ed)

The response from Australia came some 11 days later, as follows:

DEPARTMENT OF TRANSPORT
FORTITUDE VALLEY ETC.

8 September 1988

Dear Sir

I refer to your letter of 25 August 1988 regarding the issue of Traffic Offence Notice No. 4057045-4.

Your comments regarding the issue of the above mentioned Traffic Offence Notice have been noted, however the enforcement of the traffic laws, which are designed for the protection of all road users, is the responsibility of the Police Department.

The Commissioners for Transport cannot adjudicate as to whether any Traffic offence Notice should or should not have been issued.

However, a procedure exists under the Traffic Act whereby a driver who disputes the accuracy or validity of a Traffic Offence Notice may request the District Superintendent of Traffic to reconsider the matter. If dissatisfied with the District Superintendent's decision, the driver may elect to have the matter determined in Court before a Magistrate.

I have, on your behalf, forwarded your correspondence to the District Superintendent of Traffic for his attention and adjunction. The District Superintendent will contact you direct in this matter.

Yours faithfully
(NF Kent)
Commissioner.

Followed a fortnight later by this letters from the Queensland Police Department:

20 September 1988

Mr R Norcliffe
4 Austhorpe Gardens.
LEEDS LS15 8TE
UNITED KINGDOM

Dear Sir

I acknowledge receipt of your letter dated 25 August 1988, concerning the issue of Traffic Offence Notice No. 4057046-4 for an alleged offence of "Exceed the Maximum Speed Limit".

I wish to advice that the circumstances surrounding the issue of the Notice in question have been examined in conjunction with representations made by you, and I have directed that the penalty involved be waived.

Your cheque for the amount of thirty-six (36) pounds) is returned herewith.
Yours faithfully

MAPurcell
District Superintendent-Rochhampton Police District

In due course I learned that photocopies of my letter had been exposed to many state institutions in Queensland – but care must be taken not to meet up with Laurel & Hardy next time I'm up their way!!

There was an amusing footnote to this when upon our return from this wonderful trip, wife, myself and Australian hosts, Thelma, Norman and their son partook of a Chinese meal in Sunnybank.

We ordered our meal and drinks and after simply ages, our drinks finally arrived. Accidentally a brand new rookie waiter overbalanced his tray of drinks straight over my head – with froth in my eyebrows and hair this was too much for friend Norman who collapsed in a heap on the floor with laughter. His wife and my wife were slightly more controlled – their son was mortified, the waiter petrified. Eyes rolling mouth open he desperately needed an 'open up the floor' get out.

Laughter was further ignited by me trying to wipe my face with my own shirt instead of their tablecloth: 'serves you right for wearing that maroon shirt which exactly matches the tablecloth' howled Norman.

Then Thelma's guffaws because the beer in my ears 'reminded her of a spirit level'.

The restaurant had other problems and after waiting ages for our starters, we ate the ones given to us in error by another waiter which should have been delivered to the next door table! We were so hungry we were half way through them before the mistake was noticed. The other people immediately got up from the table and left in disgust. Could all this really have happened in a single day?

# Chapter 4

# That's our 'Van

The caravanning interlude for us lasted about a decade, taking up most of the 1970's. Initial trials at Matlock in Derbyshire and the Dales, followed by regular Cornish crusades ultimately led to the beckoning of the Continent and a venture into South West France. All these were so successful that the pinnacle of ambition was then realised - a haul down to Estoril in Portugal.

The combination at that time was a 12 ft Sprite Alpine and a Datsun Laurel, the latter having recently replaced the much loved and vaunted Austin 1800. The 'Van' by now was approaching 20 years of age, but sound and adapted to accommodate more that the usual 4 people. Our plans for the summer were simplicity itself. Three of us plus tent, caravan, surf board and extra kitchen sinks would unite in one week's time with 5 teenagers who would fly out to Portugal to be met at Lisbon's airport and main railway station on two consecutive days.

So, in good English weather, we journeyed to Winchester and Southampton, across to Le Havre aiming for Bordeaux sometime late on the following Tuesday evening. Everything went well - connections were made, routes negotiated and at about 5.00 pm we approached Bordeaux. The tent was packed in the boot with luggage for three, Nancy squeezed into the back alongside all the inevitable extras, whilst the caravan itself was not entirely weightless; needless to say this distribution of weight couldn't have been quite right! Approaching Bordeaux, then taking a sharp tight turn before a bridge which was closed for repair, then hitting a diversionary road which was badly rutted, there was a loud crack. "Is that our caravan?" asked stricken wife, answered almost immediately by the sight of it alongside us!

We could only watch in horror stricken amazement, as, with sparks flying from the now rampant tow bar, we once more drew ahead of her to see her break left and come to a mind boggling juddering stop against an 18" high kerb. A kerb which prevented something like a 20feet drop into a car park below! The combination of circumstances which *could* have occurred are too horrific to totally dwell upon for long - we were, paradoxically incredibly fortunate.

In an instance we were surrounded by enthusiastic, determined young French lads who detoured traffic, set out warning triangles, and blazed a number of hazard lights. Furthermore, together, we pushed the victim down the road and into the aforementioned car park, to survey the damage, with excited French comments and plentiful 'Mon Dieus!"

Miraculously it was a severe near side dent which actually affected the toilet compartment of all places. A stand up visit necessitated severe trajectory to the left - a sit-down visit, a hapless slide to the right. See what I mean? Such problems however were in the future, - what did the present hold?

Nothing inside the caravan was damaged - a few items had been dislodged and the main problem was to reconnect the

7 electrical wires. It's an ill wind, but years ago when on a trip to Wales I had allowed the electric cable to drag - severing it neatly in the middle. Repair had been a quickie - 7 electrical connectors, yards of insulating tape and bingo! This quickie was still in place prior to setting off and the new cable breaks were all at the electrical connectors. Could I patent this safe fail device I mused, as new connections were made 'red to red' 'blue to blue' 'yellow to yellow' etc, etc, etc..?

Our new found friends in adversity patted us on the back, shook hands and departed leaving us to consider the options. Carry on. Collect a new van through the 5 star insurance we'd taken out? Rest up whilst still shaken up? Or curl up and die? Really we hadn't any option but the first one, because we had to be in Portugal by Friday evening to meet the kids.

In total silence we connected up using a couple of wire coat-hangers as a safety chain (Real caravanners didn't always have safety chains in those days). We negotiated Bordeaux and drove on towards the forests, now being frequently flashed by French drivers objecting to my bright if dipped headlights; we hadn't really intended any night driving unless absolutely essential and weren't properly prepared.

Eventually an appropriate forest location was found and the van left hitched to the car whilst I went to light up the gas mantles after turning on the gas bottles. The smell of gas inside was immediately noticeable. "Quick switch off the bottle and search for leaks," came my frantic cry, as with torch in hand I carefully examined all equipment and pipes beneath for fractures. Nothing to be found except by good wife who discovered the cooker grill had been left in the 'ON' position, - no problem when the source at bottle is switched off, but distinctly unhealthy otherwise.

Of course, needless to say, all the 3 gas mantles had disintegrated, presumably on impact, and replacements needed fitting by torchlight. This we proceeded to do but no-one felt much like eating and we settled for an early night, rising by 6.00 am and being back on the road an hour later.

To say that we were the objects of curiosity from then on in, is something of an understatement. It was a wonderful conversation starter, and the incredulous looks of admiration eventually gave us a kudos we scarcely deserved.

A good example for this was the Thursday evening stop-over in a remote medieval hill town somewhere off the Zarrogosa main road. Curious onlookers promenaded in turn to witness and proclaim at our battered Sprite Alpine. We sneaked off to the single bar sprinkled with goats and chickens and 'Wuthering Heights' in black and white on TV. The owner's son could speak good English so we berated him with information so eagerly sought concerning our predicament, and on return found quite a crowd surrounding the unfortunate caravan, all vociferously expressing their sympathies and undoubted admiration with respect to our adventures.

The journey wasn't quite finished in terms of incident. A final overnight stay, just over the border in Portugal was disturbed by a group of people coming through the wood. Grabbing wooden mallet hammers, bread-knives and a tin opener we waited as they passed us by. However they were only obtaining  better vantage points for the town's fiesta fireworks displayed below, we'd had enough fireworks for a while thank you.

Similarly an anticipated 'short cut' between motorways looked to have saved us miles on the map. Unfortunately it was down and then up a 1 in 4 mountain with a radiator almost boiling, hairpin bends consistent in their frequency, and hampered by a small Fiat struggling before us. We could stop for nothing and no-one. A group of woodcutters were scattered off the narrow road as we lay on the horn; small branches, twigs and cutting gear was simply exterminated as we went onwards and upwards. We simply dare not stop. The summit when it arrived out of the mist was superb, so was the cuppa to again calm jangling nerves - were 'incidents' never going to end?

A flat tyre necessitating a caravan wheel change approaching Lisbon, a failed headlight and failed AA replacement were as nothing compared to what we'd gone through and as we settled into our campsite on the Friday evening *'achievement'* was foremost in our minds.

Teenage party No. 1 were successfully collected late that same night, my daughter exclaiming in the morning, "Look at our van" (but not being so suitably impressed as others had been upon hearing the story).

The remainder of the holiday was lively and not incident free, in fact it continued in its hilarity. Early on the Sunday morning, Nancy and I needed to go into Lisbon from the large camping site - security guarded - to collect her teenage daughter and boyfriend. We started the engine and began to quietly drive off - to be immediately apprehended by two burly guards shaking their heads with fingers to lips. It transpired that no traffic movement was allowed between certain hours of the night. Explaining our dilemma with appropriate watch pointing, train noises and role playing the panicking teenagers, we managed to finally convince our men and get out of the compound - but only by the four of us pushing the Datsun through the campsite in total silence accompanied by hysterical suppressed giggles from Nancy and myself. The 'Sound of Music' revisited we decided, when retelling the tale.

We needed to be at the station for 6.00 am - we'd done it - but wait, the station clock showed 5.00 am. For a week we had travelled one hour out of time - no wonder the roads were so empty each morning and people were just going out as we retired to bed. Why the camp guards had been peculiarly awkward we now understood.

By the way, the shape of the van had been affected by the crash and the bunk beds (my side) no longer fitted on the return journey. Despite bricks and buckets beneath it, I eventually retired to the back seat of the Datsun for uninterrupted sleep. A fractured exhaust in Madrid mended with a baked bean tin and gum- gum in a huge golden recently cut cornfield on the outskirts of the city, were about the only other 'technical' problems encountered on that particular trip.

## Chapter 5

# SOME FILEY FROLICS

Spiralling house prices, a very low outstanding mortgage and professional promotion conspired a re-mortgage situation and the consequent purchase of a 'pent-house' apartment at Filey, North Yorkshire.

Don't be fooled by the 'penthouse' bit, granted it was six floors high and towered over the famous Crescent; possessed magnificient sea views towards Flamborough in the South and Filey Brig in the North, but pretty basic it was and far from 'penthouse'. But it would afford us many happy hours with our friends.

However, it was extensive - two very large bedrooms, a split level lounge and a wonderful dining room/kitchen overlooking the North Yorkshire Moors - needless to say, any improvement to this had to be D.I.Y, and memorable D.I.Y occasions some of these turned out to be.

I've mentioned the split-level lounge, well this I did all my myself. It raised the window end of the room by about three feet and allowed access for 6 easy chairs and a coffee table to be located there. People called it Roy's stage although I did put a rail around it to prevent accidents, and only occasionally performed there!

Friends invariably accompanied us on weekends, and very often got stuck into my D.I.Y schemes. Can I recall a classic case when Peter and Les offered to help me put in a new kitchen window.

Remember we were 6 floors high, working off the fire escape balcony, in comparative safety but we had, nevertheless, to be fairly cautious with tools and debris. (Only last month I had kicked my lump hammer over the edge, fortunately without any disasterous consequences, and even a fairly large piece of glass too – good job Filey is a quiet place.)

The old window came out relatively easily and the white plastic framed new one fitted admirably; to say that it was measured by yours truly. All that was now needed to complete the task was a bag of ready – mixed cement to point the job lot in. So, off I toddled to the hardware shop, Church street, Filey, to buy the necessary ingredients.

Remember now please, that I was working alongside two very practical men, an Architect and an Engineer to boot, and they cannot escape criticism for what followed. Well, the ready-mixed was added to water, to the required consistency, and we only needed about half of the bag to complete the job. We all had doubts about the strengths of the mix – it was distinctly yellowy – and my comment that 'if this is set by next week I'll show you my bum' was greeted by jeers and appropriate comments. Well the job seemed a 'good'un' and I had to return the following weekend. A quick insertion by the screwdrive caused all the 'mix' to fall out and needless to say it was sand! The prospect of my exposed bum was eradicated.

My experience of 'ready mix' cement in bags – perhaps yours also – had always been just that – 'ready mix'. So in high dudgeon, I marched back to Filey's hardware shop to complain that the 'ready mix' was in fact solely sand – and I dramatically pointed into the old-fashioned brown bag to confirm this.

'That's right Sir, that's definitely sand'. What a relief.

'But Sir, if you turn the bag upside down', which he proceeded to do, 'you'll find a smaller bag of cement, which is actually at the top of the bag, if you open it the right way up, that is!'

All this said with a deadpan face, whilst I felt about 6" tall – the shop was busy. I left totally aghast at the stupidity of us all. It wasn't much of a comforting comment which assured me that I wasn't the first one to fall for this. Did I really get 'ready mixed' or was it 'ready to mix?'

Another memorable Filey event was the fitting of the front lounge windows – this time without a hitch, although to see my friend Peter (another Peter this time) gallivanting, squatting, working on a 2 feet wide ledge without a hand hold, still brings me out in a cold clammy sweat.

I ventured out onto that ledge quite some time later with a huge rope tied around my ample middle, one end of the rope tied to the banister rail and bring eased out by another friend equally fearful of heights. No good. I got about half way along, knees knocking in terror, before cautiously coming back. Those corner windows were never ever washed in 7 years.

A toilet semi-collapsing into the apartment below through rotting floor boards. Quite splendid, for me, fitted units and other D.I.Y jobs were successfully dealt with during our time at Ebor Court. But perhaps my most endearing memory of Filey – we rarely go back now – is a night at the pictures.

My common denominator for loneliness is Belle View Street, Filey on a February night, and it was a February half term evening, in the early 1980's when we decided to see 'Excalibur' at the local picture house. Talk about a one man band. The fellow who sold the tickets then sold the goodies and also saw us to our seats. When there was no-one else at all inside the place it was difficult to understand? To cap it all he was also the projectionist, why did he bother?

However start up time, six juveniles downstairs and two pairs of adults upstairs, were at least some company for him, making it all reasonably worthwhile.

'It's won't run with just us in will it?' queried worried wife.

'It's got to' I retorted, and so it did.

Certainly the most rewarding night was a Good Friday gallon of whisky win at the local, and the memory of Tommy and I taking it in turns to carry it home. 'Suppose we're mugged'? said Tom "If we are, just drop it on their toes and scarper" came his wife's response. Happily no such misfortunate was likely in Filey – times there were precious and always incident blessed.

# Chapter 6

# Bulgarian Gems

Bulgaria in the mid-1980s was certainly different than present-day but a whole series of comic situations, many of which were associated with the political machinations of that period, made this quite a unique and memorable holiday. Where better to begin but with a number of juicy situations?

In those days the holidaymaker to Bulgaria found themselves in a pseudo-situation at resorts tailor-made for the Western Europeans, but generally excluded to the rank and file Eastern European - give or take the odd party member or two. Thus "Sunny Coast", "Golden Sands" and such like, came into being - delightful enough villages but without any local flavour whatsoever.

The usual holiday rep., "welcome drinks" scenario expanded upon several areas of mutual interest and concern, including beach protocol, the dire consequences of changing hard currency other than in official money changing booths or banks, and presenting tokens for all food and drink within the complex and elsewhere. It was these three already clearly identified which were to create most fun. Let's deal with the beach protocol first of all!

On arrival at the beach one found neatly lined up sun shelters, the first two rows being earmarked for the Western tourist, the Eastern bloc proletariat being consigned to the back rows. Should there be no number tag attached underneath this shelter, one claimed it. One simply squatted there until the life-guard, cum beach organiser, cum film-star, cum everything else, arrived to issue you with a ticket, and to extract his payment.

Yours truly and partner found such a sunshade on the front row, neighboured by friendly West Germans from Munich and Stuttgart respectively. Before very long we were interrupted by an enormous man-mountain of what transpired to be a Finnish holiday maker.

"Mine." Finger abruptly pointing into the roof of the sunshade.
"No, mine." An equally emphatic response from me.
"Mine." Re-iterated the unknown Fin.

This time a resigned shake of my head, and a dismissal of the matter by turning to the wide-eyed neighbours, to chat irrelevancies. To my total disbelief, this led to the adversary walking off down the beach, apparently cowtowed.

The relief was short-lived as he returned accompanied by the handsome lifeguard and general beach supervisor, and a similar conversation ensued - almost a carbon-copy of before, in fact.

"His."
"Mine."
"His."
"Show me the ticket then to prove it!"

Now beginning to lose my relaxed holiday mood so early into the break, I watched as the Fin proceeded an elaborate subterfuge of going through his beach bag for the ticket. Soon the contents of his bag were strewn on the sands. All to no avail, and with a series of shrugs and grunts both men departed. As they did so, a polite ripple of applause rang out around us. It transpired that the previous tenant of the sun-shelter was a loud-mouth, in Finnish of course, a drunkard and a breast-groper. There were a few of these around - breasts, not gropers - as the official attempts to enforce a cover-up were not too successful.

I've mentioned the life-guard as a man of many parts. He was also the illegal money changer anxious to get his hand onto any hard currency he could. Some of his "parts" looked deceptively handsome but only because all his illicit dealings were stuffed down his trunks. When, inevitably, I wanted to change pound notes the amount of cash (notes of course) stashed below was unbelievable, with little signs of any of the anatomy peculiar to that part of his body. What would have happened if he'd had to rescue anyone from the sea really is food for thought?

On a serious note, he requested desperate help in writing to his English love, living in Warrington. I helped him frame a simple letter of love and care, feeling a little like an intruder as I suggested the words and formulated his structure. I was only too pleased to post the letter for him back in the UK. His simple ambition was to come to England and marry his girl. I often wonder if he ever did.

On the subject of illegal money exchange, it was only a few days later when standing on the edge of the water, that an elderly Polish gentleman sidled up to me.

"English?"

"Yes."
"Like to change money?"

Oh no not again - everyone was after hard currency it would seem, including the men in long, dark coats who frequently stepped out from behind trees on the way home.

"Well not today thanks, I'm OK at the moment."
"When then?"
"Let's say Sunday morning - we're always on the beach here."

There followed a conversation about the price of whisky in Poland, its unavailability except from Barioski shops with hard currency, the difficulties of beating custom's checks and the severity of the punishments if caught. Similar conversations throughout this holiday gave a terrific insight into the corruptions and heartaches of the Communist system.

To continue however. Sunday morning duly dawned. We were comfortably ensconced when the Pole - whom at first I didn't recognise because of the incredibly dark glasses he was wearing - squatted by my chair. There followed one of those brief but bizarre conversations I will remember for the rest of my days.

The Pole - from an acute corner of his mouth.
"Mine," (his money)" is in my hat."
Pause, equally furtive looks and a sense of panic from me.
"Mine is in my top pocket." I replied. Actually it's where I always keep what little money I have on me at any time!
"When I take my hat off my money will be inside - take it."

Imagine his horror when I responded by simply taking my money out of my pocket and giving it to him! I think he envisaged the folded newspaper, Castella Cigar box or vacuum flask. Who the hell was looking anyway and all for something around £5?! I never saw him again after that. I think I was too great a security risk.

Bulgaria also blessed us with two sets of life-long friends. Gill and Ian currently living in retirement in Liskeard, Cornwall ,and Viv and Glen a couple younger than our own children, living in Mansfield. The former couple were staying in the same hotel as us so stimulating conversations over late night drinks, and long games of Chess with Ian into the early hours were a lovely end to long, lazy days.

Ian's tendencies are to the left and thus his decision to establish his beach base at the rear, amongst the proletariat, was felt to be politically correct and despite some jesting and rude comments from me, was maintained with some dignity. He, however, had a delightful last laugh when a massive Black Sea storm on our penultimate night washed up so much sand that our beach shade finished up badly buried, so that only about 18" remained above sand! Cap in hand we asked them:

"Can we sit with you two please?"
Followed by graceful acknowledgement of course. We'd often pass Ian, a keen runner jogging his way to the huge water splash - an activity he enjoyed several times a day.

Viv and Glen were evening companions for a meal or dance or just a chat. A lively handsome couple, they were full of life and fun and walking out as a foursome despite the age-gap was always exhilarating - although the same couldn't be said of all the dining outs.

I've already mentioned that everything was paid for in "tokens". Well if you dined too late anywhere on the complex you really were *too late*! If the meal quota decided for that evening had gone, even by 7.00 pm, then it had really gone, and neither waiters nor chefs had the slightest interest - except maybe just one.

Wife and I had taken a lovely forest walk before coming across a beautiful restaurant surrounded by mini -lakes, expansive gardens criss-crossed by numerous bridges. It was not late - around 7.30 pm - but the restaurant was virtually empty. After a glance at the menu we ordered a steak and a fish. Our doleful waiter returned in due course to apologise that neither steak nor fish was available.

"Sorry Sir, not available."
"Have you been busy?" I enquired.
"No Sir, that's the way it is."

Gradually the hangdog look of Manuel of Fawlty Towers took over, he grew visibly more uncomfortable as I probed the situation.

"OK then, we'll both have chicken."

Several minutes later after some altercations from the kitchen he re-emerged,

"Sorry Sir, no chicken either, or sausage or pork!"

All this said looking more and more agitated, shuffling from foot to foot and beginning to paradoxically draw our sympathies.

"Alright," said wife, surprisingly restrained, "we'll have whatever you can conjure up for us."

At this evidence of care and commiseration he shuffled off and some sort of meal eventually arrived. This was palatable, if unexciting and ordinary. After a tasty sweet, I proffered payment and a tip. He was visibly taken aback, distinctly shocked and acutely uncomfortable.

"Sir, I cannot take so much money for the way you have been treated and the food you've had," he cried.

From then on he regaled us with the weaknesses of the system, the lack of national pride, the unworthiness of the local Bulgarian leaders etc, etc, etc. It was a somewhat mollified duo who returned to base after paying at least something towards the meal. Never before or since have I encountered a waiter who has castigated his own restaurant and its food and turned down money for the same - including his tip.

He probably thought we English were incredibly tolerant or incredibly daft.

So much then for Bulgaria and its moments of sheer magic, cheap but beautiful pink champagne, rich relationships - two superb nights of food and Chateaubriand steaks, which were out of this world, and lots of laughter. Often directed at ourselves maybe, but with new-found valuable friendships securely established.

# Chapter 7

# Maltese Cocktail - Please Sir

In 1980 we took another minor plunge, along with friends, and bought what we believe was a bargain apartment in a block of 36 residential apartments. Superb sea-views across to Comino and Gozo (Malta's sister Islands), splendid gardens and reasonable pool size, made 'purchase day' something to be proud of and to remember.

With purchasing friends and others, there have been moments of humour and worry often entangled at the same time. Regular visits have established firm friends and acquaintances, favourite local habitats from Marsaxlokk in the South to Mellieha in the North and very importantly local restaurants. It was during time spent in such, over a period of several years that a number of owners suggested bringing a team of schoolboy footballers over, on what would be a mini-football tour.

Talk maybe was cheap but as the then Head of a deprived, disadvantaged school in Huddersfield I thought, what a tremendous opportunity for some 14/16 year olds this might present. On the backs of numerous assurances from umpteen Maltese sources promising 'exchange' conditions for the students and the use of our apartment for the staff, we cajoled, worked, played, begged and threatened until all the money was raised.

Actually we had a secret weapon - one which our industrial partners and local press loved - we had a girl at Centreforward! Not just *any* girl but Samantha, a superb player, who, despite a few problems along the way, went on to play football for England's Women's team. I digress. Gradually and painfully it became patently obvious that, for whatever reasons, the staying in local homes wasn't going to happen; this was depressing and surprising because the Maltese are not known for inhospitality. Without homes to put our youngsters into we had then to consider selfcatering - and obviously raise more money for food. But, a Fairy Godmother was at hand - Mario, an owner of an apartment on our complex. Mario offered two apartments in the name of Anglo/Maltese co-operation for October Halfterm week 1988. These 15 young people and 6 'staff' were to share three large apartments close together and with full facilities.

We duly arrived at Mariner's Court to discover that the Fairy Godmother had turned into a Wicked Witch. He was nowhere to be found. A frantic phone call from yours truly.

"Mario, Roy here. Which apartments are we in?" Long pause.

"Roy, did you not get my letter?"

"What letter?"

"A letter saying I can't manage the boys".

A long, long unbelievable silence from my end, indignation, two thousand miles and nowhere to sleep, and a desperate need to re-think the situation. However matters were quickly resolved by our English friend Janet, who managed several local apartments. She duly despatched cleaners, negotiated a minimum rent and settled a patient group of youngsters, all crammed into my apartment, into respective 'halls of residence'.

Mario of course arrived; apologetic, transparent - he had let-off the two apartments. Money beats co-operation every time it would seem. I told him politely to go away; I could sort out the mess myself.

Other contacts were more than generous. Cut price mini-bus hire from Tony Mandall - until recently owner of Buggibba's Chinese restaurant and cut price meals at 'Misty Blue' owned by an International footballer; therefore, with lots in common. Our favourite eating house 'The Incognito' owned by our good friend Michael Tanti, (long admired by wife for his Italian looks and definitive style), went even better, a complete meal for all of us - a magnificent gesture.

On that Wednesday evening the 15 young people, immaculately turned out for dinner, swarmed ahead of we slower moving adults and en bloc swished through the doors and disappeared. Good God, what would they be up to as we scurried after them? Amazingly all were calmly seated around tables; Michael had guessed their identities. He then calmly took orders for 19 Spaghetti Bolognaise, one sausage and chips and one egg and chips!

That was the verb for the week 'swarmed'! They covered every inch of St Paul's Bay as a cheerful, awe-struck, laughter-filled unit. The bonhomie they created with other holiday makers, the number who came to see us play, the local press building us up really did create a special feeling. Above all, the number of people who stopped us, the adults, to relay their opinions about the group's attitude, friendliness and goodwill was gratifying.

'They're a credit to the town and school'

'What a great bunch of kids'

'You should be very proud of them'

We were!

What then of our female footballer in all this? Well, news of her presence had spread far and wide and Samantha was a keen target of attention and speculating. Not only by the spectators but by all the opposing centre halves to boot.

The first game, on surprisingly lush Maltese grass, was a Sunday morning affair at Marsa. Almost a typical Sunday morning back home, but with temperatures in the mid-seventies neither Samantha nor the team put a foot wrong, winning by three clear goals. Another match on the same pitch, where I seriously underestimated the opposition by fielding a weakened team against Naxaar was a sad loss. But the cokes, beers and crisps back in the village hall, high on a hill, more than compensated - especially when a typical Maltese power cut enabled us to 'dine' by candlelight.

Another defeat on the cement and pebble pitch at Mellieha where heavier, older boys took few prisoners resulted in severe grazings and bleeding knees for a number of players, but not Samantha who was closely marked - was it too close you might well ask?

Well the next game, yes it was! This was a match against what transpired to be a Maltese Youth team, big, strong, aggressive, cynical. In old fashioned terms for wife and myself, 'dirty buggers'. An officious referee who wanted to write all my team's names down - the match had no official status - let blatant thigh-high tackles pass and all of the team including Samantha really copped it.

Good wife could rightly stand it no longer, rushing onto the pitch to remonstrate with the referee, in good old fashioned Yorkshire language and to sympathise with the players.

"Madam, you must leave the field".

"Who do you think you're talking to".

"Madam!" - now stupidly waving a red card at her which didn't mean a thing.

Intervening I too strode onto the field and did something I rarely do in my life - pulled rank.

"Your refereeing is a disgrace to football, you've no control and are allowing too much nastiness. Unless you improve I'm fetching the team off".

"You can't do that".

"Oh! but I bloody well can".

"I won't let you".

"Oh! yes you will.  Know why?  Cos I'm the boss, the big boss".

Things calmed down after that, although - Sod's Law-it was a Huddersfield player who eventually lost his cool and plonked one on the end of the opponent's nose.
"Sorry Sir", he said directly up on joining me on the touchline.

"I couldn't cope with it any more".

Two other natural spontaneous remarks stand in my memory.  At half-time after asking Samantha how she was faring she said nonchalantly,
"I'm OK Sir, but that centre-back keeps feeling my tits!"

Matthew, our superb Afro-Caribbean captain, shortly to sign professional forms with Huddersfield Town, came across to me at the height of one of my passionate outbursts and put his arms around my shoulders.

"It's all right Sir, really it is, we can handle it".

His calmness, dignity and composure left we adults just a little shamefaced.

The game was actually played on a subsidiary pitch in the National Stadium at TA'QALI under inferior floodlights. Throughout it was very difficult to pick out our black players apart from their white topped socks which shone in the gloom.

"Sir" said red-haired Alan, a very nervous goalkeeper, "I can't see Chris and Matthew"; even he had similar problems at his end.

Torn socks and split shorts were all testimony of the battle - this game being ironically set up by the Catholic Church footballing authorities. Needless to say the next game was cancelled when I firstly criticised Father Patrick for showing not the slightest interest in our visit and secondly for the conduct of his team. One minor consolation was that Samantha at last had her own personal dressing room.

The last game was in Victoria, the capital of Gozo - again a muscular youth team. Perhaps our finest performance of the tour was given here in a 3-2 win. Despite the slamming of dressing room doors and being miserable losers the Victoria lads joined us for a cheerful aftermatch gathering at Marsalfarn - a favourite haunt of ours. Again behaviour was impeccable and praised by visitors.

We caught the last ferry home to Marfa, the lads and lass enjoying a 7-aside in the ferry hold where our two minibuses were the sole occupants. Several weeks later back at home the Head of PE asked what had happened to one of the matchballs. A bashful John, coincidentally in our presence, admitted that it had been 'lost overboard' at that time, probably beaching in nearby Libya.

A final serious and sobering memory abides where Mark sitting across from me in the aisle on the plane home suddenly collapsed with a minimum pulse rate.

An ambulance was scheduled to meet us at the terminal, although by this time he was semi-recovered and being sick. After whisking the party through the inner realms of Manchester airport the doctor pronounced Mark sound in wind and limb.

"Mr Norcliffe, whatever have you been doing to this lad, he's totally exhausted".

"I know the feeling" I responded sheepishly, "but you try stopping teenagers working and playing to their limits on such a trip".

There and back again - we wouldn't have missed it for the world, even though it took us all a month to recover.

## Chapter 8

# STUDENTS RULE OK
## *Part 1*

1996 'there and back again' took us around the world in five remarkably tranquil weeks - Bali, Queensland (again), New Zealand and Hawaii. Nothing in the way of incident or freakish happenings to report! I'm beginning to believe these days that a holiday or visit abroad isn't really worthwhile unless it's incident packed. There were, however, two trips associated with work when I accompanied thirteen students to Southern Ireland, then a further six to Athens in Greece. Lets take the former made in March as a starter.

Funded by European Commission money, our prepared brief was to present a piece of Children's Theatre in Education to eight Primary schools in County Cork; these schools being situated around the town of Fermoy and Cork City itself. Arrangements had largely been made at the end of 1995 (see Chapter 10 which outlined the fun in getting there for my 'recci') and travel was from Holyhead to Dublin then down to Fermoy where thirteen students and two staff were to be accommodated.)

Now our Irish partners, soul mates, sharers of unique experiences, etc, etc, were supposed to be a local college who, for the sake of charity, must remain nameless. I expected some sort of greeting or welcome party when we drove up to the former convent, now converted into a sort of monstrous residential educational establishment, but only John, a warm-hearted, extrovert young warden, was there to greet us with hot soup, sandwiches and cakes.

Apart from a few inches of extra dust here and there, bare metal gleaming on lights without bulbs, lights with bulbs that didn't light anyway and a bed or two which collapsed on being looked at, we felt welcomed enough, but perishingly cold in a great, spooky rambling building, itching to show us a ghost or two.

We had been promised a mini-theatre to rehearse in, but that would have meant the college acknowledging our presence and so we set to final rehearsals in an ice-box of a chapel - inhabited at one end by off-putting statues of, amongst others, the Virgin Mary. As one Beeston lad remarked:

> "I'm not keen on her looking at me Sir, wherever I go in this place, she's everywhere - inside and outdoors."

It was apparent that my charges were abysmally lacking in any knowledge of the local faith, when later the next day, on a first date with a local lad, Clare apparently insisted:

> "I'm a Christian by the way, not a Catholic" - out of the mouths of babes!

Gradually, the students became more and more uneasy about our accommodation, but more and more assured as we polished up our performance piece for its first presentation at a village school some six miles from Fermoy.

Incidentally, another negative response from the college came when we were refused access to some make-up. Only a mad dash to Cork with Jo, my colleague, double parking in the city's main street for 15 mins, whilst she did the business, and an equally mad dash back for the opening session saved the day.

The village school in Ballingandan was only three classes small - the Headteacher cleared one which doubled as his office, the children cleared another, putting all desks and chairs outside and in the third room. We managed in the second room with limited - extremely limited - performance space. Hoping to be about ready to begin, I sensed a problem elsewhere and returned to the Headteacher's room, which was by now, a communal dressing room and make-up room, to discover Jo, some cast members and others busily trying to eradicate marks from the carpet. Someone had unwittingly got black make-up on their shoes and were depositing it all over Ireland, it would seem.

With hands on hips, the unsmiling young link teacher from the Fermoy college growled:

> "Roy, this will not happen again" - warning looks from Jo as she paused in her grovelling.

> "Can't you see it was an accident?"
> "The carpet will never clean" - toss of head.
> "Yes it will, and if it doesn't, then my own college will pay for it being done professionally."

Somewhat mollified, but with the Headteacher winking and giving me encouraging signs, we eventually got off to a rousing start.

Gradually, however, the cold and damp and probably tiredness took an almighty grasp of us. Four times in fourteen days I traipsed to the doctor's for medication; four times the doctor came to us when my charges seemed too sick to move.

As the saying goes though, 'the show must go on' and on it went indeed. The show itself featured Yorkshire and recounted the adventures of a group of animals forced out of their natural habitat by environmental pollution and the greed of developers. A resident vet might have been of further value as quite a number of animal characters on some occasions had difficulty with voice and movement. At one school 'rabbit' was left behind, fast asleep and picked up on the return journey. Fortunately, the cast knew their lines backwards and everyone else's too, for that matter, so the missing or 'silent/voiceless character' was, as a consequence, of little handicap.

So much then, for the real content of the Irish trip, the Leeds' students presenting work of the highest calibre and ensuring that the reputation of the Performance Arts Department remained undimmed. But what happened elsewhere, you might well ask, in some anticipation ............ well!!

As has already been determined, the Holy Family Centre was a massive place, a rat-run of corridors, side-rooms, toilets and bed-rooms. It also housed the twice weekly meetings of Alcoholics Anonymous, who sometimes failed to go home, finding instead, a nearest dormitory or bed to spend the rest of the night. This was all well and good if the other side of former convent, but next door to the girls' dormitory or in one of our own boy's bunks was not on. I personally found the threat of these fellows negligible, but try convincing 17 year olds familiar with the UK's social problems, that this is the case.

The problem was an 'unlocked door' policy which again put the frighteners on the students, and no amount of convincing about culture, normality in these parts, safety or personal security was going to change their attitude.

Our visit, purposely, coincided with the famous - to the Irish, that is Co Waterford Drama festival where, for two solid weeks, plays were performed in the Ballyduff Hall. I took it in turn to take small numbers to a play, and these mainly continued, with adjudication, until way past midnight. As a result, return home times were quite late indeed.

John used to light us a superb fire in the main lounge, but on each return 'something' would have happened and students would be crouched by the fire awaiting our return.

> "Adam saw a white figure earlier tonight".
> "Christina and Caroline heard slow footsteps on the top floor".
> "John says two men in the pub were overheard threatening to burgle us."
> "We locked the door Roy, but it's unlocked itself."

Impervious to it all, I expected something of this nature each evening and it was therefore, with some surprise, one night when we arrived back to find no one up. The fire was past its best, but untouched logs scorching in the hearth was most unusual.

On visiting the respective dormitories we found the students en-bloc, cowering in one room. Can I take up the story of events as unfolded by one of them?

"We were chatting by the fire as usual, frightening each other with various stories about the 'Holy Family Centre', when we saw a face framed in a window." (This window was adjacent to a corridor which ran through to the Chapel.)

The story continues:

"We screamed out and found the face to be that of Charlie, the odd-job man, (an apt description incidentally) who thought it a great joke. After a while, however, without warning, the same window shattered and fell into the room. We all dashed upstairs, hid here and here we're staying."

Well, in truth the window had smashed and there was no immediate logical explanation as to the cause of this. Perhaps it was already cracked, perhaps it was under previous stress. I tried to re-assure with all manner of half-hearted explanations, but I didn't really convince anyone, including myself.

However, our time in Fermoy was almost done and I attach a newspaper article featured at the end of this chapter which succinctly recorded our visit. Taking part in the town's St Patrick's Day parade was a real highlight. We garlanded the mini-bus, paraded on top of, inside and outside the bus in full regalia to mountains of applause.

The relaxed final four days which incorporated greatly improved weather on the West Coast more than compensated for Fermoy deprivation. We were able to do and see ordinary everyday things so that all the various ailments were largely improved by the time we set sail from Dublin for England and home.

# Leeds drama group on tour in Fermoy

**A group of Leeds students recently spent a most productive two weeks in Fermoy and took part in the Patrick's Day Parade in the town.**

All were drama students undergoing a one year Diploma in the Performing Arts at the Leeds College. Associated lecturer on the course, Roy Norcliffe, who travelled with the twenty or so students, says that this course is very much a prep course for further drama studies and gives those involved exposure to every aspect of the Arts including acting, directing, lighting, sound, stage management etc.

Park Lane College has loose links with Coláiste an Chraoibhín and during their stay in the town they resided at the Holy Family Centre in the Presentation Convent. This trip was far from being one simply for leisure, because the students have written their own play and during their stay they performed this piece for many of the National Schools in the area. In all they undertook eight performances in schools in Ballindangan, Castlemartyr, Kilworth, Dungourney and Ballyduff. Further performances were staged in Tallow and Lismore and in the Holy Family Centre itself. Roy Norcliffe says the play has an environmental theme dealing mainly with the way that many wild animals are driven from their homes by man. The problems that ensue for such creatures are then dealt with.

The students themselves say that the performances have gone down particularly well in the many National Schools in which they performed. They say they were made to feel very welcome by all the principals involved and for that they are very thankful.

While they have thoroughly enjoyed their stay, the second half of the trip has seen many of the group fall victim to the cold Irish weather. On the day of this reporter's visit sneezes and coughs were the order of the day and hot drinks and tissues were very much in evidence.

Nevertheless, Roy says, the whole trip, which is being sponsored by the European Commission, has been enjoyable if somewhat hectic at times. He paid particular praise to Fiona McDonnell from Coláiste an Chraoibhín who he said had put much time and effort into ensuring that their trip went off well.

*Part II*

Students, six in number, four girls and two boys; venue: Athens; season: mid-June.

The brief for the trip was to acclimatise and settle in the students before they embarked upon an intensive package which involved working with top theatrical directors, actors and choreographers. My stay was a brief six days before fellow lecturers and colleagues took up responsibility for a further fifteen days.

Coincidentally, the first day there happened to be my 60th birthday - certainly in 1936 the thoughts of such prospects for my parents would have been non-existent. However, there I was charged with the onerous task of 'settling in' and introducing six young people mesmerised by their presence in such an environment and by the sheer magic of their fortuitous situation.

We eventually began my birthday by strolling through the PLAKA and ascending to the Acropolis and spending time admiring the superb views on a typical early summer Greek day. Luncheon called and we located a typical tavern some way below the Acropolis. Students are not the most compatible of diners, being too picky and hesitant for my liking, with appetites like the proverbial sparrow. However, not so today. Each ordered a significant respective local dish of their choice and asked a couple of very elderly strolling players if they could play 'Happy Birthday' to yours truly. They couldn't! However, a brief chorus of the tune established some sort of basis and 'Happy Birthday' was rustily rendered by a fiddler and accordionist. Magical!

Later we explored further tourist attractions, although an after evening meal celebration was cancelled when we were called to a 10.00 pm meeting with the Greek theatre professionals - a meeting which went on until 2.00 am. Exotic people, intense and friendly, and for me, a bottle of rare Raki as a birthday present.

A day on Aegina and a belated celebration the next night after partaking of delicious pizzas were further long standing memories. As we all strolled arm-in-arm down the wide boulevard back to the hotel it was difficult not to feel enormous contentment and real bon-homie.

A last night-cap at a roadside bar was certainly called for and a Jameson whiskey seemed a nice birthday present from the group. As we settled down a police-car mounted the pavement and parked alongside us. Panic! What had we done wrong; were we that bawdy? No problem, all they really wanted was a quick beer on a hot night and a chat to the girls.

Richard said,

> "Roy, do you think we could ask for a dramatic picture, me against the car being frisked with a gun on me?"

> "Er....er....er", I responded. "I suppose so."

Richard's languages being first class, the first policeman eagerly understood and so the picture was taken. More friendly conversation ensued before the policemen finally asked for the girls to send pictures of themselves back to the policemen in Athens on the girls' return home.

Sally then went downstairs to the toilet and shortly after the sound of a gunshot came from below. Out of the door of the cafe shot Sally - onto the pavement.

> "Christ Roy - he pulled the gun on me and fired it, I've nearly shit myself!"

> "Only blanks, only blanks," a smiling policeman re-assured me.

At that moment a second shot came from below, shortly before a smiling Nathan and Richard emerged.

> "Great, fantastic, what an experience! I fired a gun", exclaimed Nathan, shaking hands with the second policeman.

Enough was enough. I called them to order and we retired - better not let the boss back at College see these pictures, I thought.

The remainder of my time sped by. Idyllic time in the company of six caring, committed young people whose conduct was exemplary and stimulating. Final goodbyes were said, but birthday memories abound.

# Chapter 9

# TO RUSSIA WITH LUCK AND FUN

Fired by Pasternacks 'Doctor Zhivago'; and the perceived vast wilderness of white, it was always an acute wish to see Russia, and Moscow in particular, in the depths of Winter. Not in Spring or Summer when probably, if not undoubtedly, there will be colour, delightfully fresh visions, together with an atmosphere of conviviality and ready smiles. No, it had to be Winter, although cheerless, slushy and grey it would well be in the Russian Cities

The New Year of 1986 was the appointed time, when Mikhail Gorbachev's 'Perestroika' was beginning to be more than just a whisper and where public voices were increasingly criticising the system – it didn't take a great deal of later discovery to understand why.

It began very badly! An overnight stop for the four of us at Gatwick, then promptly on board an Aeroflot jet, on a bitterly cold 27th December (actually colder in London that day than in Moscow) we sat and waited – and waited. Eventually the plane doors were reopened someone's luggage was loosely stuffed up front and two more people embarked. But still we waited – our flight slot had been missed!

By now, 2 1/2 hours late, we eventually took off after being presented with an uneatable lunch of horrid cold meats, trying to hold together disintegrating seats and consoling one fretful wife who had discovered she had no safety life jacket. Yet we duly arrived in Moscow's main airport unscathed.

I said I had wanted snow, and there it was – tons and tons of the stuff piled high in irregular masses with more gently following on the top.

Disastrously more interminable delays. Because we were late, the airport baggage handlers had all gone home and had to be recalled from their beds, or Vodka, to sort out 120 or so very disgruntled travellers. Passports seen, faces grimly inspected, luggage, in several cases roughly handled and also inspected, at long last we arrived at 'The Rouska' hotel, near to Red Square, but several miles from the originally brochured hotel.

More delays as rooms were allocated, plans for morning made, and the despairingly short amount of possible sleep time was calculated. (Don't forget we had also lost a further 3 hours to the time clock).

However, most of us made the 'City Highlights' tour, later on the Bolshoi Ballet, The Moscow State Circus and other superb cultural delights, but it was the bits in between that really grabbed the memory bank in later years.

Let's take our outdoor pool swim for the first example – close friend Peter and new acquaintance Alan both knew of a heated outdoor pool some half-mile or so from the city centre. Alan had visited Russia previously, often at this time of year, and was convinced he knew his way around. We couldn't really miss the outdoor heated pool even in the dark as very shortly across a Park we located a high witches' couldron brewing in the distance. The effect of the water at something around 82 degrees F meeting a night air temperature of –9 degrees caused enough 'fog' to blanket a small village.

After trying one locked unattended door after another, we at last gained entry into the changing rooms. Excessive giggles and funny looks were at first confusing; we didn't look that funny. Eventually it became clear as a large pair of breasts lumbered through carried by an unperturbable Russian lady that we were unfortunately in the ladies changing rooms. Mumbling apologies, beating hasty retreats and with never, a backward glance (well perhaps one) we at last found the mens' section.

The 'fog' seeped everywhere but taking in our surroundings we seemed to be in a pre-revolution, Victorian equivalent of a typically tiled swimming baths–the sort of pre-war construction and decor I was familiar with in pre-war Sheffield buildings – including hospitals. A large, very ugly woman watched the three of us changing quite dispassionately until she surprised me somewhat by tugging at my swimming shorts – shorts not trunks mind you. Did she want to see me naked, did she want to buy my shorts, did she not like me wearing them in the water? I didn't wait to find out but followed the others along the darkest, longest, and most eerie tunnel I'd ever encountered. The tunnel which we pre-supposed led to the water.

Imagine three grown men, two of them middle-aged holding hands inching their way in almost total blackness to be met by peculiar noises and a large thick rubber door which went under the water at its bottom end.

'I'm sure the weird noises are dolphins' whispered Alan – what's more he meant it!

'Don't be stupid' I replied 'this is a public swimming pool'.

'How do you we get in though?' questioned Peter, an individual usually of sheer common-sense. Even he was shaken by the situation.

Eventually sanity did prevail and we presumed that by diving *under* the rubber door we'd make the pool alright. Ah, but who was going to ascertain as fact this presumption? Who was prepared to clout their head even on the bottom of a rubber door? Who was prepared to meet the unknown on the outside of that door? After numerous pushing and pullings and frequent cowardly moanings, Peter decided to give it a go, popping up almost immediately to confirm that the rubber door only submerged a few inches into the water.

It was, and still is, the weirdest swim of my life. Echoey, silent, vast, warm – providing you didn't expose your cranium – the atmosphere was unique, the pool perfectly circular with frequent ropes across it, for the less strong swimmers. To see the clear stars above, feel the bitter night air yet the velvety warmth of the pool was absolutely magical. We were enthralled, encapsulated in something unique and special.

'Chewing gum?' was whispered softly in my ear.

'Pens, jeans, watch, - me buy?' in someone else's ear.

Well these were not the sort of goods any of us regularly carried around, even out of the water, so the Russian boys received disappointing responses to their advances.

Perhaps the whole affair lasted two hours at the most – it seemed a lifetime of experiences. Frequently we recalled how long that particular holiday seemed. It was only a week but seemed so much longer, and we theorised that – rather like children – we experienced so many new and different things that time magically slowed right down.

Two other travellers with us had apparently arrived in Moscow with inappropriate documentation and spent the night under guard and locked in their bedroom before obtaining British Consul help to rejoin the rest of us. So they also had plenty to tell and various anecdotes were bandied around from a variety of sources.

New Year's Eve in Red Square was additional fun and quite amazing in concept. Prior to strolling to Red Square, we had seen the magnificent State Circus, like demented children ridden the immaculate beautiful metro and celebrated UK New Year with a few bevies at 9.00pm Russian time.


After having hysterics watching the barriers rapidly threaten the mens' privates, if they delayed too long after inserting 5 kopeks, we boarded a metro underground carriage to an unpronounceable destination. Picture the scene, if you can. Ten or so Western tourists in a relaxed happy reflective New Years' Eve mood confronted by dour Russians travelling home. Two of these were young lads, one of whom had a canoe oar upright by his side. Welsh Jean, one of our party, grabbed the oar, mistakenly believing this to be part of the carriage handrail-as you do! The tube took off at great speed, up and along came the oar followed by the two lads hanging on for grim death. Hilarity from us, no response from any of the Russians, until, alighting at the next stop, our two young lads collapsed in a rolling heap of laughter on the platform floor. Thank goodness for that we opinionated, we were becoming increasingly worried at the seriousness of it all.

The New Years' Eve celebrations at a time when East-West relationships were far from tranquil and the actual 'seeing in' of New Years' Eve 1986, trapped beneath the Kremlin Wall and St Basils' Church can never be surpassed, should I live another 60 years.

Immediately prior to New year itself, the many International groups enjoyed banter with the armed Red soldiers numerously positioned around Red Square. Although 'Niet, Niet' was expressed to members of our group as the Gordon's gin was unpocketed ready for action, it didn't really matter at all a few minutes later as 12 o'clock struck. Thousands of champagne corks popping, the sound of multi-languaged 'Old Lang Synes' (their equivalents I supposed) and the sight of Red Army officers, of beaming soldiers, and civilians of every Nationality in total harmony of rhythm and dance was patently moving. However, our most abiding memory was being seized by Mongolian strangers extraordinarily beautiful – if gold toothed – and forming our own spontaneous East/West line dance. Literally crossing minds across the supposedly great divide. Pictures of wife and Ann in the arms of beaming soldiers frequently nudge us into the strong emotions of the occasion reminding us that it did really happen, otherwise credulity would be stretched to the limit.

Did that magic really exist? All the people, all the camaraderie, all the fun, within the beleaguered Red Square, and a heap of champagne bottles come daylight.

The Bolshoi Ballet, overnight luxury train to Leningrad as it was then, the deep cross-country snow, the beautiful 'Summer Residence' and 'Heritage' are all further lasting memories. As are those of the Aeroflot refuelling at Riga where we were escorted by armed guard to the glassy clinical airport for a paper cup of aerated water, before being escorted all of the 30 yds back to the air craft. Who would have wanted political asylum anyway?

## Chapter 10

# 2 MILES AN HOUR - MODERN DAY TRAVEL!

No, this didn't happen in the days of horse drawn carts, or in a pair of walking boots but latterly in November 1995. How did such a bizarre situation develop - you may well ask?

A business trip to Ireland actually; rare for me these days. Dutiful wife dropped me at a local Leeds Station - Crossgates to be exact, shortly after 4.00pm and in good time we anticipated for the journey to Manchester Airport. Forget it! The train connection incoming from York was delayed some 40 minutes due to 'signalling problems outside York'. It was with some irony that from being favourably positioned for a decent seat I was just able to squeeze a standing space because of the huge volume of commuters; by now gathered for later trains, but who gleefully took mine. Well, it was only a 15 min standing situation to Huddersfield, then matters became immeasurably better - or did they?

Without doubt something was amiss as the train proceeded - oh so gently - to Manchester Piccadilly, but arriving some time around 6.35pm I was still comfortably placed for my 8.15pm Dublin flight. The train usually stands a little while in Manchester Piccadilly but when someone got on asking 'If this train went to Newcastle?', then another questioning a 'Huddersfield stop' my confidence began to wane - despite the fact that the questioners quickly bustled away. Alarm bells were ringing but silenced somewhat by a train tannoy announcement that all airport passengers were to alight, and further informed to proceed to Platform 11. For a train? Not likely!!! In crocodile file we were led to the front of the station to a double decker bus whose destination front proclaimed RAIL REPLACEMENT. Already those of little faith had abandoned the rapidly sinking ship - those like myself prayed on; 7pm by now and flight time merely 75 mins away.

'Rail Replacement'! This was, calling at all points between Piccadilly and the airport - 6 in all - passing through housing estates and past salubrious homes, but please do not ask me their obscure names. Low flying aircraft were constantly in the ears and sight but never it would seem bringing us closer to our destination. But, yes, at last there we were - all of us desperately wanting Terminal 1 but having to go to Terminal 2. It was a train station you see, and Terminal 2 was the train station. The fact that everyone wanted the former was totally irrelevant.

Mad dash then back to Terminal 1 - daren't wait for public transport, even free, at this stage. I arrived panting and dishevelled about 15 mins before take-off time, to be smilingly informed that take-off was to be early and literally in two minutes. Obviously, I looked elated at the grand news and needed to be brought back to stark reality.

'Actually, sir, the Dublin/Leeds flight had to be cancelled due to an aircraft which was not airworthy. We have brought the passengers to Manchester and are diverting you' - yes, you've guessed it - to Leeds!!!

A forced smile denied my real feelings, with respect to the unloading, picking up and refuelling still so close to my Leeds home.

There then we ultimately were. Taxiing down the Leeds/Bradford runway some 5 hours after leaving home - a mere 10 miles away. However, we miraculously arrived in Cork 'bang-on' time as we say in Yorkshire, and I'm still not sure how or why. The return journey? Well that's another story, but why any company should want to buy Railtrack beggars belief.

# **Chapter 11**

# **A Real Paella**

August 1992 saw an overland trip to the Costa Del Sol, Plymouth, Santander (an expensive first class cabin!) and then the direct drive to Granada with stops - one overnight - at Toledo, Madrid and Burgos. Nothing over exacting or indeed over-exciting at this stage but the scenery, towns and general sights along the journey were distinctly memorable.

After Granada, a right turn following the coastal road led us to our destination, Bellanmedina, some way to the west. Here friend Alan, now the owner of two lovely apartments at the Santa Cruz, was to await us for a 9 day stay with him and then a 4 day drive back along the De Sol and Brava coasts and up through central France to Calais for the three of us. That was somewhat ahead however.

Alan has many friends, including those of the fairer sex, indeed the darker variety and unfortunately, we cut short his amorous entertainment for that night, arriving apparently a day earlier than we had forecast. Silly, thoughtless me! Invalided out of the fire service in his mid-fifties, Alan is a larger than life character who has actually seen and done more than your average fireman - with due respect to this admirable breed of men. However, not best pleased, he now had little option but to admit us and curtail his wooing and cavorting for the time being.

Our first few days were lazily spent sunning, swimming and eating before a round trip to Saville, Cadiz, Rhonda, Porto Banous was undertaken. Memories of standing in reputedly the oldest bullring in Spain; watching in horror a speeding car on the hairpins up to Rhonda lose control (after overtaking me) and start to speed back down the hill towards me still out of control - before finally stopping - were only surpassed by a huge burst water hose on our motor, just before arrival back at base.

Now a short piece of hose shouldn't be a problem, should it? Especially with a Renault company as big as Barnsley just up the road. Don't kid yourself! Despite all our efforts (and theirs, so they told me) the said hose failed to materialise. Alan decided to visit a small back-street garage who promptly cut off the required piece from a section hanging on a wall, fitted it and charged me about 500 pesetas.

"No problem Englishman" he said, particularly as I gratefully and huge heartedly doubled his asking price.

However, we did experience slight overheating problems still and a careful watch was taken of the corresponding temperature gauge throughout our journey home - happily problem free, as it transpired.

Alan had postulated the plan to literally follow the Spanish Coast road virtually all the way to Marseilles before turning North. It was pointed out to him that *we* had jobs to get back to and that we preferred a Yorkshire Christmas to a French one; we'd use the Auto routes and stop off either overnight or as time permitted, during the day, wherever we fancied.

Our first overnight stay was Mahaco in a beautiful English owned bungalow close to the sea. A luxurious stop-over this, easy access for a swim after a long day's drive, a relaxed sumptuous meal in a delightful fish restaurant in the mountainous outskirts put us well on our way to the next planned stop somewhere around the area. Again, we plotted an advantageous stop, but our anticipation proved all in vain.

We made such good time moving ever Northwards that a 2 hour sojourn, some sun-bathing and a swim at Benidorm seemed really added value and we duly parked up and headed across the beach to the sea. June and I chose a vacant sunbed and parasol; stuffing, as is our habit, goods and chattels safely underneath us whilst Alan flopped down some 10 yards away.

"I'll take yer picture you two", declared Alan, squatting in front of us, camera at the ready. Snap, snap, snap, before returning the 10 yards back to his little pile of belongings.

"Hey up Roy, have yer got me wallet?"

"No Al. Why?"

"Yer must have - me wallet, me money, me credit cards."

Mad search amongst all our belongings, but unbelievably, they'd gone and no-one appeared anywhere near us or indeed, in the immediate vicinity. To this day, between us, we cannot be sure whether this was an audacious theft or if that wallet was dropped between the car and beach. Alan was convinced however, that he had it with him.

'Sod it Alan, we're going to have a quick cooling dip before we report to the police station', I decided. So we did both.

The police station located, details passed over, credit cards stopped, (including one still in a drawer in Leeds) a loan agreed between us and Alan, it was a chastened trio who re-commenced their journey - about 4 hours after arrival. The shrugs, gesticulations, 'Si Sis' well behind we had to settle for a roadside, essentially lorry-drivers', hotel. Our planned coastal deviation was dismissed due to the lateness of the hour.

By the middle of the next day we were well into France on target for a rendezvous with two members of my then teaching foreign language staff who would either be just married by the time we caught up with them; or about to be so, by the local mayor of a minute village near Corcassone. Mike had given me a map which directed me from the old town to the gite they were renting for the whole of the summer holidays. After circumnavigating Corcassone twice, then seeking English speaking help, we thought we'd cracked it.

Yes - a bus stop, then a tiny hotel, turn right across a ford and after one mile their gite would appear. Not so. Again, I sought help and map in hand, leaving the other two in the car, I walked up a long, high, privet-lined drive towards a sophisticated mansion. I could hear laughing somewhere ahead of me and also the sound of more exotic merriment. Clearing the privet hedge I glanced to my right to see emerging from a glorious swimming pool an equally glorious female, a bronzed goddess of a woman - completely starkers!

This wonderful creature was side-on to me and obviously focused on a second bronze body also climbing out of the water beside her. He too was naked, enviously endowed and both were immediately wrapped in each other's arms. What a situation and still I hadn't been spotted, rooted to the spot, feeling a voyeur for the first time in my overdressed state of tee-shirt and shorts. Was it appropriate, I thought, to present both myself and map at this incongruous time? I scarpered, not hurriedly I must emphasise, not in an undignified way, but simply by ducking behind the privet hedge, fully expecting voices of wrath to be following me as I skulked down their driveway.

To this day I wonder what and how I would have coped with asking for mundane directions in such close proximity to the whole of two total strangers. Would I have averted my gaze and kept my cool, or would I have dithered? Would I have been arrested as a 'peeping tom'? No, in this case discretion was the better part of valour.

After this little escapade we were no better off than before but, after turning the car around and making further enquiries, we were told of our mistake. Believe it or not, there was a second series of bus stops, small hotel, right turn and cross the ford. Spotting a recognisable car at the rear of the gite I went into what seemed an utterly deserted residence. Halfway through I suddenly thought 'what if Mike and Tes are equally nude out on their own Sun Terrace.'

Before I could contemplate this outlandish coincidence I was through and onto them, sunning yes, but nude no. It transpired that we'd missed the wedding by 24 hours, but this didn't prevent a superb local village feast, bottles of celebratory red wine and a late, late night negotiating numerous fields and lanes to avoid any local gendarme.

I suppose the remainder of the journey passed uneventfully. Another overnight stay in Cher where Alan forgot our borrowed alarm clock, duly and kindly returned a month later to Leeds, an overnight ferry from Calais and my being too tired to drive after we'd passed London.

"I'll sit up front with June and support her home" offered Alan as I stretched out on the rear seat.

By Northampton apparently, our combined snoring drowned out the tapes.

# Chapter 12

# Fancy A Pint?

Based in a small hotel about 20 kilometres from Prague, shortly after the fall of Communism, a good pint of beer or lager was hard to come by in the small hotel where we were based. Either no-one was interested enough to serve or the stocks were too low to suffice a two coach party strength.

One evening whilst one half of the tourists went local to see some country Czech Republic dancers, the remainder promised to locate a mysterious pub reputed to lie somewhere in the extremely remote country village - where electricity hadn't yet graced their streets.

On our return from Prague the recci. party confessed that, despite their best intent, no such pub could be located. The hotel management played it dumb and daft, yet rumour persisted that a small hostelry did exist.

The following evening thus saw twenty people armed to the teeth with torches. searching the village lanes for a pub. All to no avail - nothing was to be found. Suddenly, a bicycle light emerged from the late October gloom and a poor young lass was accosted by this large group of people intent on their beverage.

"Pub?"

"Beer house?"

"Drink?" Accompanied by wonderfully varied mimes as people imitated drinkers.

"Ah!" A wave of the hand presumably meant, 'follow me', which we did.

The young girl eventually laid her bike by a garden gate and disappeared into a house to soon emerge with a friend, who was equally clueless as to what we wanted. Finally, shakes of the head meant that mission impossible had failed, so we all dejectedly loped back to the hotel, having to face a dismally closed bar there. A game of cards ensued, the evening passed, convivially and at a really late hour three intrepid tourists burst into the room to explain gleefully, "We found the pub - it's extraordinary, we'll take you all tomorrow" - and so they did!

What a 'pub' it transpired to be. Actually, it was a two-room cottage, where one stepped over the threshold into what might best be described as the kitchen part. A sink, shelf, stone slab, were its main furnishings and apart from a Johnnie Walker's whisky and a Polish vodka, no other spirits were visible. But there were barrels of Pilsner lager and we quickly ordered before taking our drinks into the 'lounge'.

This was a scruffy, tattered place with old wooden chairs, overturned barrels or boxes for tables, a toilet smell which blasted the nostrils and a dense fog promulgated by a dozen Czech chain-smoking roadworkers.

So there we sat drinking the most delicious draught Pilsner - the factory was only 10 kms down the road incidentally - whilst the cost of the stuff never entered our heads.

However, eventually we called it a day; asked for our 'account', which was presented to us on a piece of torn-off cardboard!

Somewhere in my household I still possess this priceless piece of paper, entirely unintelligible hieroglyphics, soiled and unreadable. It translated roughly thus:-

| | | |
|---|---|---|
| 4 pints of lager | = | £2.00p |
| 2 Vodka and oranges | = | 50p |
| 2 Coca-Cola's | = | 20p |
| | Total | £2.70p |

Payable in Kopecks, we had to check the cost to see if indeed, we weren't ripping somebody off. We weren't, but a generous tip to the hard working land-lady, coping brilliantly on her own, was testament to a superbly, funny night.

Compare this with a lunch-time meal with new found friends, Lynne and Dave from Coventry. Really, we only wanted a snack and a beer and when I saw people disappearing into a hole in the City wall, obviously some sort of hostelry, the rest followed me. This we later found out was one of Prague's leading restaurants - formal, stuffy, penguined waiters and very - very expensive. Promising ourselves just soup and a bread-roll, we were inevitably tempted by succulent hoers-derves and latterly, sweets of a most delicious nature. Whilst it cost a bob or two, it was certainly a blast from pre-war times and again an experience to savour. It really was especially atmospheric.

As Lynne kept on telling me - "I'll never follow you into a hole in the wall again!"

# Chapter 13

# AN OLD ENEMY

For as long as I can remember, there and back again certainly by bus, sea and car, equated to travel sickness purgatory. Sunday School trips just after the war meant trips to Barnsley the 20 miles return journey being worth 4 vomit points. A journey to town was worth two points (return) a trip of about 8 miles in total.

Things gradually improved into adulthood, although a Blackpool Yacht trip, a Filey Bay self-yachting occasion with a friend and a Hong Kong ferry did cause me to succumb.

However, 'Sea Legs' have been a boon - with them I seem infallible - so that uncertain as I might sometimes be on land and sea, generally speaking, I've been reasonably sickness free. This even included a 12 day Caribbean Cruise, where I 'sea-legged' it at the slightest possibility of rougher seas.

Air Travel is it seems, my travel forte. Even with obvious turbulence I cope admirably, but the smaller aircraft provide some possibility of vomit points. I think of the small sea-plane ducking and weaving around the Great Barrier Reef, and a small plane attempting to land in awesome thermal currents at the Masai Mara Game Park in Kenya when I just managed to 'hang on' - as did profusely alarmed wife.

Forget "it's only in your mind, if you don't think about it you'll be all right", this really is a myth, and a fallacy.

I recall with pride surviving a gale in the Irish sea one September when ferries didn't even chance it for three days from Cork, and we had to drive up to Dublin to make it home. This was the only ferry leaving Ireland, the others being cancelled because of the sea conditions. Wedged horizontally on a seat, drugged to the eyeballs with 'Sea Legs', washed down by generous doses of whisky, I survived. I was incapable of driving on from the other end mind you when we embarked, so once again fair wife came to the rescue.

Another October crossing from Zeebruge to Calais was certainly very fraught but 'Sea Legs' again did the trick quite effectively, so that sausage, chips and beans was also tackled with gusto. I was prevented from having a pudding however, upon seeing June gaining her own personal vomit points at the aft end of the ferry (it's better to be sick for everyone concerned at this end of any boat), having forgotten to take her own 'Sea Legs'. Making sure I had taken my medicine this was a first for her, as she normally revels in sea voyages.

Recently I ventured a boat trip from IBIZA to FORMENTERA - a most unwise decision. Left on my own at the back end of another working holiday, June having returned to England the previous weekend, I decided to go on this particular day in early June. The day previous had been still and calm, but this particular day dawned grey and fresh - still what the heck!!

Several mistakes were made on this fateful day:

I    Going from San Antonio Bay and not Ibiza town (the crossing transpired to be 2 ½ hours compared to half an hour by hydrofoil).

II   Having the temerity to board the small boat because there were insufficient numbers for the much larger boat.

III  Not realising the extremes of the wind outside the protection of San Antonio Bay.

We sailed on time hugging the East Coast of Ibiza then plunged across fairly heavy seas to finally dock in harbour. Convivial Yorkshire company, a splendid sighting of 'South Pacific's' (the musical) famous 'Bali High' rock, and extraordinary views of my hotel from the sea were high-spots of a journey which, at the very worst, left me simply needing a coffee and a toilet - in reverse order actually.

Four hours on a delightfully different Island where I pedal cycled for 4 hours before duly returning to the boat were soon to be confined to the thought dustbin as I pondered the return to San Antonio.

As I drank a small beer at a quayside restaurant, the wind quickened even more, the flags blew stiffly, the posts leaned alarmingly and to cap it all, grey thick squally weather enveloped us. 'Senors, please, we must sail' shouted the skipper, pointing to the threatening skies. How I wished I'd either stayed there or taken the faster, bigger ferry to Ibiza Town and then a bus back to San Antonio.

We sailed!  Alas as soon as we turned into the open sea I knew there was no way I could possibly survive two hours and more of this little lot.

Tossing, bobbing, falling sideways, first one way then the other, the sea hypnotising me - there being no land to see or focus upon - the inevitable had to happen.

Fortunately I was 'aft', a policy already recommended, and thankfully the boat was not full.  I also had in my possession a large beach towel so that somehow I kept my dignity - I think.  Whether I went unnoticed in my agonies or whether fellow passengers were being studiously polite, I'll never know, or care, for that matter.

However, an alarming potential disaster at sea was a further incident which occurred during this particular voyage.  A German woman passenger decided to move seats at the very same instant that the boat pitched alarmingly to the starboard.  Grabbing a vertical pole, an integral part of this heap of junk, as was quite natural, suddenly the whole pole came away in her hand.  Reeling helplessly backward, she sailed through the air landing on the side seats, but half sprawling over the boat's rail.  Fortunately an equally savage roll back to port brought her upright, and from having legs high in the air above her she mercifully righted into a more dignified position.  One thing for sure, I couldn't in any way have raised myself from my state of debilitation to have thrown her a life jacket.  I am just thankful the choice did not have to be made.

The rest of the journey and day is best forgotten.  No dinner, several tonics and an early to bed for me.

# Chapter 14

# MY BEST DAY OUT

Whether these reminiscences can be faithfully described as an actual "best" day out might to some people, be arguable. Nevertheless, respectively and indisputably the six protagonists involved will always classify the first Sunday in August 1985 as our most outstanding memory – masochists that we might well be considered.

It initially began as a result of strong desires to travel the Leeds/Carlisle railway link – before its threatened closure! The debate and lobbying to keep the line open at that time seemed to be at its peak and we actually decided to try and discover for ourselves precisely what the fuss was all about, and indeed take the ride before it was too late.

In our case, with Daughter married the previous weekend and safety ensconced on honeymoon in Malta, it was with somewhat lightened shoulders that we convened at Leeds City Station equipped with all the necessities – little dreaming that some of these would not be returning home!

The journey to Dent station and lovely stroll down to a Dent hostelry was typical and enjoyable in full sun, warm winds and with excellent visibility. A good leisurely lunch, a saunter through Dent and a glimpse of the Sedwick Memorial Stone before the serious stuff of an afternoon's walk to Ribblehead Station to rejoin the train for the evening journey home. Easy!

The intention was to spend the remainder of the afternoon within the triangle of Deepdale, Whernside and Blea Moor with time no object and weather seemingly set fair.

The 'steady' incline was coats off stuff, until almost unnoticed the sun disappeared, the weather closed in and the temperature dropped like a stone.

Initially the rain fell as slight drizzle but inexorably increased in tempo and volume, until as we reached the highest point of our walk the water was rushing down to us and the conditions became absolutely appalling.

Ribblehead Viaduct seemed to be the only possible shelter from the elements as we slithered and slipped our way downhill towards what had rapidly grown into more than a gentle beck below. Inevitably something had to give and it was my thermos flask as I went flat on my back, where at least the haversack afforded some protection. Several ridiculous minutes were spent finding extra stones upon which we could ford the once very shallow stream. Why we didn't simply walk across – we were totally wet around the feet by now anyway – is another matter.

The shelter of the Viaduct was reached – except that it wasn't really shelter because the rain blew everywhere – and certainly pieces seemed to be missing, was it that safe? Across a field was a small barnlike structure where it might, just might, be a little drier. Alas to no avail, the cow muck was virtually a foot deep and fluid to boot – not exactly condusive to Tuna sandwiches and wedding cake.

Onwards we trudged – "Let's just get the next train home"-
except that it was still one hour and a half to the next train.
Cold, wet and famished four of us amazingly resided within
the Station's disused Gents urinal – there wasn't even a
waiting room accessible. This after turfing out four sheep to
make room for us. The 'Ladies' would have been drier, but
that already contained a further couple of sheep and we
didn't relish another struggle with them. Afterwards we
realised that the sheep hadn't actually opened the door
themselves and gone in, but had been shepherded there.
Guiltily we eventually got them back in, even they weren't
prepared to wander far in the conditions outside. We four
actually stood in the porcelain tray as the water was about
6" deep on the floor, it was certainly "chummy". Meanwhile
we had to try and change some of our garments, but alas all
the replacements were equally sodden, and we were
scarcely any more comfortable. The other couple from our
party had already sheltered outside 'The Station' pub along
with several other victims. A pitying landlord opened up
somewhat earlier and they composed themselves inside for
a little while. The 'urinal dwellers' meanwhile partook of
refreshments and donned slightly less soddened clothes,
balancing precariously with arms round each other to try
and keep warm. We laughed ourselves silly at the
incongruity of it all and played word games to pass the time,
which went by surprisingly quickly.

We all duly rejoined the train, finding a mass of drowned
steaming bodies, steamed up windows and compartment;
clothes everywhere in any conceivable drying spot. I knew
that my light walking-boot soles were beginning to part from
their uppers on the right foot. Walking along the platform in
Leeds City Station, the boot finally gave up the ghost,
transforming itself into something resembling a large fish,

whose mouth kept constantly opening and closing with each step I took. The boots, along with the remains of the now defunct thermos went into the bin on the station and the remainder of the walk to the car was made in stockinged feet.

It should be added that the River Ribble viewed alongside the rail track, had burst its banks in many places, and fields were flooded on a massive scale.

A hot bath for us all – separately not communally. We later joined up for a Take-away Chinese meal at the culmination of the day, making it one impossible to forget.

But, heresy to most readers, as far as we were concerned at the time, that railway line couldn't be closed soon enough.

# Chapter 15

# Cornish Rhapsody

I conclude these personal reminiscences by paying tribute to our magical Cornish holidays throughout the 1960s. I've been fortunate to see so much of the world during the last two decades but the annual two week jaunt to places such as Crantock, St Ives, Bude and Padstow will inevitably stay longest in the memory bank.

It's not difficult to understand why really. These holidays were precious days spent with our children and close friends together with their children. We only received two weeks holiday per year from the Sheffield steelworks where I was then employed - a far cry from the 13 weeks 'Education' later blessed me with. I defy any teacher to argue that compared with the rest of the workers at that time you were not over-favoured. (If you can't beat 'em join 'em I decided in 1971).

Yes, these Cornish holidays were golden days. Usually late August they were mostly sun filled and spent surfing, playing football or cricket on the beach, and sand castle building. All the ordinary things which became extraordinary as we shared the fun and laughter. Later we met up with and shared holidays with a large Manchester family thus setting up 'Roses' battles at cricket and cross-county football competitions, besides indulging in the card game 'Crib' on the beach.

Cornwall was for us another world. A long 12 hour drive then in motor cars which had seen better days by far. I know my parents worried themselves sick that we'd arrive safely and intact after 350 mile drive in A35s, Morris Travellers, Ford Anglias etc etc. We invariably did, proud as punch at our achievements comparing travel times and distances in a most competitive manner.

My good friend Roy knowing we were almost penniless and how hard we'd had to save for the two weeks away always serviced my car before departure - without taking a penny for his pains. Once and once only in almost a decade of 'old banger' travel did we hit upon mechanical problems.

Just prior to arrival in St Ives in 1968 my Vauxhall Victor (bench seats column gear change, remember?) developed pulling problems. We managed for a day or two before approaching an AA serviceman situated in the great car park at Lands End. After a cursory examination he declared the car needed servicing.

"It's just been serviced" I snapped
"Well it needs new plugs perhaps"
"It's got new plugs in, I did that myself"
"Well maybe its electrical or petrol problems"

What a Wally I thought as I left him no wiser as to the fault.

The next day immediately on arrival at the car park above our favourite St Ive's cove five of us decided upon our own investigation and decided to check the petrol pump flow. What a mistake that might well have been. Immediately the loosened petrol ignited on and around the engine block.

Panic ensued but the car rugs and small fire extinguisher we always carried did the trick leaving us amazingly damage free. So it wasn't the pump either we agreed as we took up our places on the beach, a singed eyebrow or two between us.

Simultaneously the car developed gear lever linkage problems, with the failure of a very small ring; the sort of hard rubber ring which went around Tizer bottle tops in those days. A trip to Truro and Falmouth the home of Vauxhall spares failed to produce this ring so yes, you've guessed it, we fitted a Tizer bottle top ring which certainly saw us home.

We decided to leave well alone - we couldn't actually afford any garage fees - and set off home to Sheffield with real trepidation. By nursing, cajoling, pleading we gradually limped towards Yorkshire. Driving behind a Sheffield coach which pulled me in its towpath for many miles along the M1, we thankfully reached the top of our home hill where final expiry took place in the drive. What was the actual problem you might ask? Well actually it was a blown cylinder head gasket and by this time we had an oil sump largely topped up with water.

Those were the days though. We always arrived home completely refreshed, sun browned, ready for the fray. Christmas was the next break on the horizon but somehow that didn't really matter then.

I compare those fleeting days with my family of two and the Thomson 'T' clubs, creches and Charlie chalk equivalents at many modern hotels or camp sites and think that I wouldn't have missed the company of my kids for a fortune. Working long hours often arriving home after their bed time it was a bonus to share all day with them on holidays.

Other memories flood back as I write. Brenda - our friend - blocking the toilet with a disposable nappy and me frantically stemming the tide as water cascaded down the boarding houses carpeted stairs. Mark, my son, stamping and throwing a wobbly because his ball was rapidly going out to sea and no-one, particularly Uncle Adrian, a strong swimmer wouldn't go after it. The fact that he was changed into a lounge suit at the time seemed irrelevant to Mark!

I remember too the landlady who couldn't make Yorkshire pudding and how we stuffed them into handbags and fed them to the gulls. You daren't leave anything on your plate then. Even after June and Brenda showed her, she still produced a stodgy uneatable blob.

I remember further the electrical storm which hit one year and a thunderbolt hitting a house directly across the street. The end result was of 8 people in one bed so terrified were we. The same small hotel was blessed with an incontinent puppy so that care where you put your feet was imperative. One day it ran off with Marks' jumper, Brenda made a grab for it, and caught one end, but by the time the dog had got to the bottom of the garden about one third of the garment had become unravelled. Happy, happy times. Even when precious daughter was totally soaked after falling into a pit we'd dug, just as the tide filled it to a depth of three feet. Best friend or no Adrian got a real dressing down from indignant mum.

I conclude by remembering old Ada Tozer our very first Cornish Landlady, hers being a superb Crantock Bay bungalow with just our family of eight as her lodgers. We realised she was perhaps past her best in 1963 when with cataracts troubling her eyes we began to receive mouldy bread, and unmentionables in the cabbage. Finally one dinner time as we sat around the table she patted the top of an empty chair.

"Tides up en ee?" followed by
"He's a quiet un today en ee?"
Paul the usual baby occupant of the chair was in fact asleep in the bedroom!